AF270378

Droughts

by Julie Murray

Dash!
LEVELED READERS
An Imprint of Abdo Zoom • abdobooks.com

Level 1 – Beginning
Short and simple sentences with familiar words or patterns for children who are beginning to understand how letters and sounds go together.

Level 2 – Emerging
Longer words and sentences with more complex language patterns for readers who are practicing common words and letter sounds.

Level 3 – Transitional
More developed language and vocabulary for readers who are becoming more independent.

abdobooks.com

Published by Abdo Zoom, a division of ABDO, PO Box 398166, Minneapolis, Minnesota 55439. Copyright © 2025 by Abdo Consulting Group, Inc. International copyrights reserved in all countries. No part of this book may be reproduced in any form without written permission from the publisher. Dash!™ is a trademark and logo of Abdo Zoom.

Printed in the United States of America, North Mankato, Minnesota.
052024
092024

Photo Credits: Getty Images, Shutterstock
Production Contributors: Kenny Abdo, Jennie Forsberg, Grace Hansen, John Hansen
Design Contributors: Candice Keimig, Neil Klinepier

Library of Congress Control Number: 2023948512

Publisher's Cataloging in Publication Data

Names: Murray, Julie, author.
Title: Droughts / by Julie Murray
Description: Minneapolis, Minnesota : Abdo Zoom, 2025 | Series: Natural disasters | Includes online resources and index.
Identifiers: ISBN 9781098285500 (lib. bdg.) | ISBN 9781098286200 (ebook) | ISBN 9781098286552 (Read-to-me eBook)
Subjects: LCSH: Natural disasters--Juvenile literature. | Droughts--Juvenile literature. | Drought management--Juvenile literature. | Precipitation (Meteorology)--Juvenile literature.
Classification: DDC 904.5--dc23

Table of Contents

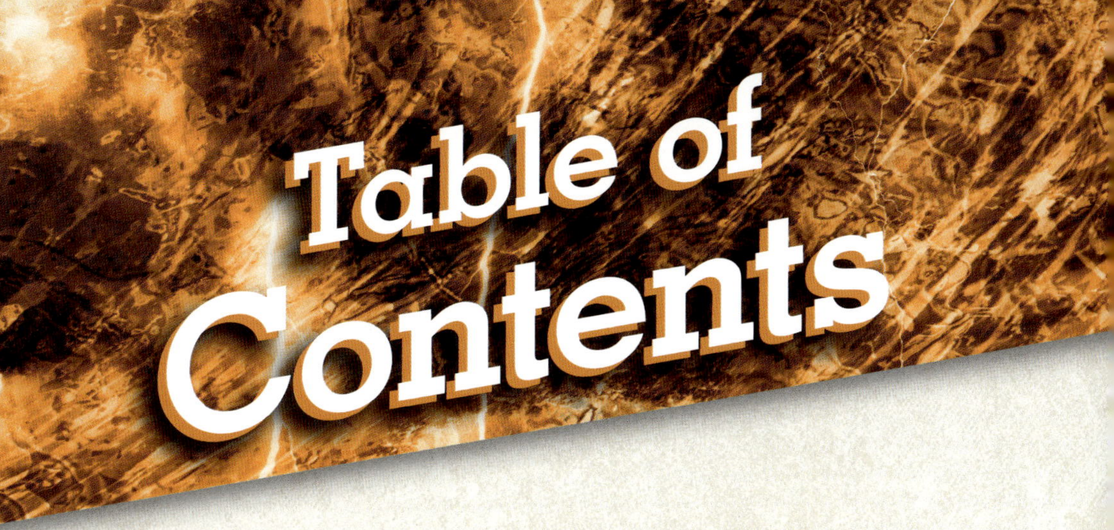

Droughts. .4

Causes 10

Effects. 16

More Facts 22

Glossary 23

Index 24

Online Resources 24

Droughts

A drought is a period when an area experiences less **precipitation** than normal. A drought can last for days, months, or years.

During droughts, the ground can become dry and cracked. Water levels in rivers and lakes become low. Some bodies of water dry up completely!

Droughts can be deadly. They can lead to a shortage in the water supply. This affects plants, animals, and humans.

Causes

Droughts are mainly caused by changes in weather patterns. The cooling or warming of ocean water and air temperature affect weather all over the world.

Climate change also contributes to droughts. The Earth's temperature has risen two degrees in the last 150 years. It is enough to melt **glaciers** and dry up lakes.

Human activity is one cause of climate change. Deforestation, farming, and overuse of water all harm the Earth.

Effects

A drought in the **Great Plains** of North America caused the Dust Bowl of the 1930s. Strong winds blew the top layer of soil off the ground. Farmers had to move to other areas of the country.

Wildfires can also be caused by droughts. Dry conditions and hot temperatures create the perfect setting. Wildfires spread easily in these conditions.

Without water, crops can't grow. This affects the food supply for people and animals. Today, droughts affect 55 million people each year.

- Droughts have affected more people in the past 40 years than any other natural disaster.

- La Niña is a weather pattern. It causes higher temperatures and less rainfall for the southwestern United States every 3 to 5 years. The area has a higher chance of a drought during this time.

- More than 40 million people in East Africa have been affected by droughts since 2020.

Glossary

glacier – a large body of ice moving slowly down a slope or valley or spreading outward on a land surface.

Great Plains – a vast grassland prairie region of North America east of the Rocky Mountains.

precipitation – snow, sleet, rain, or hail that falls to the surface of the earth, or the amount of it that falls in a given period of time.

Index

causes 4, 6, 11, 13, 15

climate change 13

Dust Bowl 17

dust storms 17

effects 8, 17, 18, 21

food supply 21

water supply 6, 8, 15, 21

weather 11

wildfires 18

Online Resources

Booklinks
NONFICTION NETWORK
FREE! ONLINE NONFICTION RESOURCES

To learn more about Droughts, please visit **abdobooklinks.com** or scan this QR code. These links are routinely monitored and updated to provide the most current information available.